$1
—IS—

MORE THAN

TIME, TALENT, AND THINGS

A New Agenda

C. NEIL STRAIT

BEACON HILL PRESS OF KANSAS CITY
KANSAS CITY, MISSOURI

10 9 8 7 6 5 4 3 2 1

Dedicated to
Ina
for her encouragement, love, and support

Contents

Foreword

More than time, talent, and things? Before I began reading Neil Strait's manuscript, I wondered how stewardship could be more than those three old standbys—time, talent, and things.

This book surprises us with a new outlook on a familiar subject. Stewardship, Dr. Strait shows us, is more than a legalistic set of dos and don'ts, more than rigid rules and *outward* obedience. Authentic stewardship requires "a deep commitment to Christ, an understanding of His Word, and an obedient spirit." Indeed, stewardship is a matter of the heart.

In these pages you will find yourself challenged, as I was, to reexamine your whole approach to life. Am I a steward of my relationships? How do I define success? Can I handle failure? A renewed perspective on these questions can be the raw material for personal revival in our lives.

In the chapters that follow, Neil Strait offers us the opportunity to enlarge our view of stewardship. No part of our world remains untouched when we become committed to minister "as good stewards of the manifold grace of God" (1 Pet. 4:10, NKJV). Join me as we begin an exciting journey. Let us embrace stewardship as life-size!

—BONNIE PERRY

Preface

Stewardship is not a contemporary buzzword. It speaks too much of accountability, restriction, and sharing, which are not popular ideas in a secular-oriented society. Exploring stewardship is the last thing some want to do, mainly because it invades the comfort zones of life.

But we must guard against thinking that no one is interested in the stewardship of life. I believe there is a thirst in the land for the sacred, deeper things of life, and that the area of stewardship is higher on the agenda of modern people than we think.

I came to a new appreciation for the subject when I first heard of Pete Rose's problems. Here was one of baseball's finest players—talented, enthusiastic, exciting, durable, dedicated. But the continuing indulgence that had gripped his life had shattered his career and brought it to an abrupt end. The press released the story about the time I accepted this writing assignment. I began to think about Pete's situation in the light of stewardship. Such questions as the stewardship of success—or failure—surfaced. What about stewardship of talent? Of course the old standby, stewardship of money, was pertinent too.

I began my research thinking that it was ground pretty well covered. This was confirmed. But I discovered that most material focused on money or things. While that is certainly an important theme, it is not the whole.

The planning for this book began to focus on the wider dimensions of stewardship. What has finally settled in my thinking is that we are discussing a philosophy of life. It is a follow-through to what we believe. It is an expression of the inner person.

What I offer here is not the last word on the subject. Rather, it is one person's perspective of a vast and important area of life. If we are to live with meaning today, we must give attention daily to this matter—the stewardship of opportunity and responsibility.

I offer these pages with a prayer that we will be challenged to give greater attention to stewardship in our lives, and in the hope that we will be stretched to faithfulness in these important areas.

Quotations at the end of each chapter are from my column, "Strait Lines," as published in *Quote Digest* across the years.

My thanks to those who have encouraged me along the writing journey. My wife, Ina, has been a good listener to my thoughts and ideas, and a constant support of my writing endeavors. My thanks to Sharon Folkert, who put the manuscript into finished form. Her efficiency and skills are deeply appreciated.

Stewardship Is More than
Time, Talent, and Things

As each one has received a gift, minister it to one another, as good stewards of the manifold grace of God *(1 Pet. 4:10, NKJV)*.

So then, men ought to regard us as servants of Christ and as those entrusted with the secret things of God. Now it is required that those who have been given a trust must prove faithful *(1 Cor. 4:1-2)*.

An Agenda for Stewardship

Money! That is the first word that comes to most people's minds when stewardship is mentioned. Fund-raising, pledge campaigns, and tithing are close behind. While all of these are factors, none is the sum total.

Stewardship is a broad subject. I suspected it was so when I began this book, and it was confirmed early into my research. On the inside cover of a recent magazine were these words: "The best things in life are not things." That, in a nutshell, is the silent message of stewardship.

Many definitions and ideas abound—all the way from "Stewardship has to do with money" to "Stewardship is caring for the environment." Both are right, to a degree. But both are wrong if that is all they propose in their definition.

There is a historical opinion in the church that stewardship has more to do with money than anything else. In fact, such opinion has been so widespread and apparently unchallenged that it is seldom questioned. Such acceptance shuts off consideration of the principle in other areas of life.

The other side of stewardship's definition is that it touches all areas of life and to some degree can best be understood and interpreted as one's total response to life's opportunities, responsibilities, and talents.

The Christian needs a new agenda for stewardship—an agenda that incorporates what is good from the old, but embraces also the new that God is teaching His people. The Christian's walk is a learning path—new light, truth, and discovery are part of a relationship with God. While the Christian's beliefs are based on changeless truths, he or she also is bringing all of life's changes into alignment with these truths. Stewardship is the process God chooses to mold our lives to His timeless truths.

Our daughter, Jolyne, buys me books for special occasions because she knows how much I enjoy reading. One Father's Day she gave me a copy of Lou Mobley and Kate McKeown's book, *Beyond IBM*. A statement leaped out at me: "A rocket . . . is on course only 2 percent of the time—the rest of the time it is correcting."[1]

Stewardship is like that. A certain part of life is on course with truth in the daily response of obedience. But more often than not, the challenges and responsibilities of life invite us to "correcting" postures. Life, then, is doing the work of stewardship—responding to truth.

Such an interpretation moves our subject away from the emphases of money and managing life's resources. It moves it into the arena of truth, where life is viewed, not from the vantage point of what one can gain, but from the vantage point of truth—what one must do, as a disciple of Jesus, to gain the Kingdom. This, I propose, is a new agenda for most of us.

The rudiments of the world have seeped into the Christian culture and theology. Centuries ago it was the Christian Church and the Christian who influenced culture. The establishment of colleges in those early years of life in America is one testimony of Christian influence. Today, it has been observed, the world has influenced the church, leaving it compromised and complacent.

Robert H. Bork, in his book *The Tempting of America: The Political Seduction of the Law,* illustrates this worldly influence on American culture. He writes: "If by vilification you can make people believe that the center is actually the extreme right, then you can get them to think that the left must be the center."[2]

When truth is not a priority, then the interpretations of

the world seem right. Secular mentality has all kinds of strategies to camouflage the truth. The agenda of stewardship is to sort out the good from the bad and to chart a course along the path of righteousness.

Ernest Boyer poses a good question for the person who is serious about this matter. In his book *The Blackboard Fumble*, he highlights this challenge for us: "We know how to extend life beyond what might have been its natural limits. The question is, 'At what point have we introduced more bad than good?' In business school we turn out graduates who know how to make money on Wall Street, but we often fail to ask, 'What is the right way to make money?'"[3]

As Christians we must be concerned about our influence in life. Integrity, faithfulness, and commitment must be character's repertoire if truth is to be honored and impact made on a secular mind-set. That the task is gigantic is not debated. Charles Colson, who makes no apologies for his concern that the church has not influenced the world the way it should, wrote this in his book *Against the Night:* "The crisis is in the character of our culture, where the values that restrain inner vices and develop inner virtues are eroding. Unprincipled men and women, disdainful of their moral heritage and skeptical of Truth itself, are destroying our civilization by weakening the very pillars upon which it rests."[4]

A right response to truth, by way of our stewardship in life, is one answer to the dilemma Colson views. It must include more than one segment of life; it involves all of life, as we shall see.

The wise steward is one who cares for today, in order that tomorrow will be safe and meaningful.

Reduced to its simplest terms, stewardship is an acknowledgment of responsibility.

Since an overseer is entrusted with God's work, he must be blameless—not overbearing, not quick-tempered, not given to drunkenness, not violent, not pursuing dishonest gain. Rather he must be hospitable, one who loves what is good, who is self-controlled, upright, holy and disciplined *(Titus 1:7-8).*

There was a certain rich man who had a steward, and an accusation was brought to him that this man was wasting his goods. So he called him and said to him, "What is this I hear about you? Give an account of your stewardship" *(Luke 16:1-2, NKJV).*

2

Stewardship Is God's Idea

A study of stewardship must begin with some basic beliefs. One of these is that God is Creator. If this is not deeply believed, then the biblical view of stewardship has no track on which to run. God, as Creator, is the reference point in the study and identification of this theme.

A second basic belief is that the Creator God has entrusted the care—the stewardship—of His creation to people, people like you and me. God has assigned each of us to be stewards over some part of His creation. What an awesome thought! God has given His best into our care. It is frightening at first, but upon reflection one remembers that God always gives grace, strength, and wisdom to accomplish the tasks He assigns. He does not promiscuously delegate care of His creation. The parable of the talents teaches us that He expects competent stewardship and final accountability. The parable reads:

> Again, it will be like a man going on a journey, who called his servants and entrusted his property to them. To one he gave five talents of money, to another two talents, and to another one talent, each according to his ability. Then he went on his journey. The man who had received the five talents went at once and put his money to work and gained five more. So also, the one with the two talents gained two more. But the man who had received the one talent went off, dug a hole in the ground and hid his master's money.
>
> After a long time the master of those servants returned and settled accounts with them. The man who had received the five talents brought the other five. "Master," he said, "you

entrusted me with five talents. See, I have gained five more."

His master replied, "Well done, good and faithful servant! You have been faithful with a few things; I will put you in charge of many things. Come and share your master's happiness!"

The man with the two talents also came. "Master," he said, "you entrusted me with two talents; see, I have gained two more."

His master replied, "Well done, good and faithful servant! You have been faithful with a few things; I will put you in charge of many things. Come and share your master's happiness!"

Then the man who had received the one talent came. "Master," he said, "I knew that you are a hard man, harvesting where you have not sown and gathering where you have not scattered seed. So I was afraid and went out and hid your talent in the ground. See, here is what belongs to you."

His master replied, "You wicked, lazy servant! So you knew that I harvest where I have not sown and gather where I have not scattered seed? Well then, you should have put my money on deposit with the bankers, so that when I returned I would have received it back with interest.

"Take the talent from him and give it to the one who has the ten talents. For everyone who has will be given more, and he will have an abundance. Whoever does not have, even what he has will be taken from him. And throw that worthless servant outside, into the darkness, where there will be weeping and gnashing of teeth" (Matt. 25:14-30).

It is evident from this parable that God does not give us His talents and His creation without thought to how they will be handled. This truth must be remembered in defining and interpreting stewardship.

Integral to these basic beliefs come two concepts that undergird the topic—responsibility and accountability. These two responses are built into true stewardship. While our society may have downplayed responsibility and thumbed its nose at accountability, we must not assume that this has lessened the biblical requirements of stewardship. It is a false premise to conclude that because contemporary thought views these two responses with compromised value, the same is true with God.

A creeping paralysis in the church world results in the use of the contemporary to interpret biblical truth, rather than vice versa. The responsibility and accountability of stewardship is no less today than it was the day God began creation. He shares His best with expectation that it will be handled with care.

Many people take a dim view of responsibility and accountability. They view such ideas as hindrances to personal freedom that do not fit into the modern interpretation of freedom and behavior. Responsibility and accountability appear too often to be prisons for the secular spirit. For such, stewardship, in the biblical sense, is foreign and forbidding.

What we must see is that the Spirit-led person is interested in freedom to *be*, more than freedom to get. That is a major difference between the spiritually-minded and the secular-minded. The secular mind wants to do its own thing. It accepts no restraint of responsibility to slow the quest for selfish pursuit, nor does it want the yoke of accountability to impede its journey.

Stewardship, in its broadest and most biblical perspective, is seeing the issues and potentials of life and its resources as gifts from our Creator God. As such, they are to be used to enrich life and to glorify Him. A good steward sees responsibility and accountability as natural responses where love and obedience are factors of relationship, rather than restraints. Because the steward loves God, treasures that relationship, and values the resources entrusted to him, the result brings honor both to the treasure and to Him.

So what is restraint for one person is relationship for another. The selfish agenda wants nothing that would deter the impulsive and sensual cravings of the flesh. A regimen of responsibility would put these sinful practices in shameful and revealing perspective, so it is easy to see why accountability is avoided. Tragically, some of the most memorable illustrations of this avoidance have come from well-known religious figures. Here were men who posed as spiritual leaders but were writing their own agendas, heated and fueled by greed rather than directed by responsibility and accountability. The weakest parts of their organizations were responsibility to spiritual principles and accountability of funds entrusted to their care. These are sad exhibits of lives run by selfish agendas.

It can be tempting to feel we are in control when the volume of things builds around us. We must understand that not only is our trust an assignment from God, but also it can be withdrawn by Him. Again, the parable of the talents teaches not only the expected care and accountability of talents but also that God has the right to take all of them from us. Years ago, Dr. R. T. Williams, in his book *Relationships in Life*, wrote this:

> The authority of a steward does not lie within himself, but is found in someone above him, from whom he receives his authority and rights. This authority held by the steward is not absolute, but relative, not inherent, but delegated. The rights given the steward may be removed at the will of his master.[1]

Proper stewardship begins with a deep sense of the authority of God. He is Creator. He is sovereign. And He is Judge. All of this must be taken into account when we write our agenda concerning our trust. Not only is God the Giver of every gift, but also He maintains sovereign authority over each gift. Joseph F. Jones has said, "The steward does not give back to God 'a portion' of what the steward owns, for God has never relinquished ownership."[2]

The conclusion of stewardship is summarized by the author of Ecclesiastes, who wrote:

> Now all has been heard; here is the conclusion of the matter: Fear God and keep his commandments, for this is the whole duty of man. For God will bring every deed into judgment, including every hidden thing, whether it is good or evil (*12:13-14*).

Stewardship, in its biblical setting, is doing the whole will of God. Included in the will of God is proper oversight of all He has given to us in terms of time, talent, and treasures. It is a big order. May our prayer be that of William Walsham How:

> *We give thee but Thine own,*
> *Whate'er the gift may be:*
> *All that we have is Thine alone,*
> *A trust, O Lord, from Thee.*

The reward for faithful stewardship is fulfillment and peace—fulfillment because one is busy doing the things of God, and peace because that is His gift for obedience. Faithfulness is not just a duty, it is a life-style. It is a response that recognizes that the blessings of God come from proper discharge of responsibility and accountability.

Recently, the youth of our church were challenged with these words: "The call to commitment is a call not to add something more to your already busy schedule, but to let go of some things that prevent you from experiencing the joy of the Lord in service."[3]

This is the new agenda for stewardship—to let go of all that keeps one from experiencing the joy of the Lord! It is the celebration and maintenance of relationship—a relationship with the eternal God.

Stewardship, then, is a follow-through of our love for God. It is putting into life our commitment to Christ. It is putting into a life-style what we believe in our hearts and verbalize with our lips. Someone wisely stated: "Stewardship is everything we do after we say, I believe."

Stewardship is one of the requirements for meaningful life. For where the sources of life are not cared for, there ceases to be available the necessary ingredients for purposeful living.

The wise steward is one who handles all of life as a gift on loan from God. Such a steward is faithful to see that all gifts are used for His glory.

Who then is the faithful and wise manager, whom the master puts in charge of his servants to give them their food allowance at the proper time? It will be good for that servant whom the master finds doing so when he returns. I tell you the truth, he will put him in charge of all his possessions *(Luke 12:42-44)*.

Whoever can be trusted with very little can also be trusted with much, and whoever is dishonest with very little will also be dishonest with much. So if you have not been trustworthy in handling worldly wealth, who will trust you with true riches? And if you have not been trustworthy with someone else's property, who will give you property of your own? *(Luke 16:10-12)*.

3

Stewardship—What Is It?

Our new agenda is to find the rich meanings of stewardship that open to us opportunities for obedient response to our Lord.

A steward, in the biblical sense is a person given responsibility for managing that which belongs to another. The parable of the talents makes this clear. It begins with the idea of "a man [owner] going on a journey, who called his servants and entrusted his property to them" (Matt. 25:14). Dr. Samuel Young, in the *Beacon Dictionary of Theology*, writes:

> Stewardship is an open acknowledgment that man is a creature who is the chief object of divine beneficence, both in creation and through redemption. From the beginning, man received dominion over God's creation both as a gift and a task. . . . Man from the outset was amenable and responsible.[1]

The word *steward* was first used in England around the year 1000. It refers to an official who controls the domestic affairs of a household. The Greek words *oikos*, meaning "house," and *nomos*, meaning "law," combine to give us the New Testament word *oikonomos*. The word *stewardship* is a translation of the similar New Testament word *oikonomia*. This refers to the management of an estate or a house.

T. A. Kantonen wrote *A Theology for Christian Stewardship* many years ago, in which he stated that stewardship "acquires a spiritual significance . . . when our Lord uses it as a metaphor to a man's management of his whole life in responsibility to God." In the Pauline Epistles *oikonomia* becomes a definite religious concept. Paul uses it in defining his commission as a preacher of the gospel (1 Cor. 9:17). He speaks of himself as a steward of the grace of God (Eph. 3:2) and of the mysteries of God (1 Cor. 4:1).[2]

Our Lord Jesus Christ gives us the biblical context of a steward, and hence, stewardship in a parable to His disciples:

There was a rich man whose manager was accused of wasting his possessions. So he called him in and asked him, "What is this I hear about you? Give an account of your management, because you cannot be manager any longer."

The manager said to himself, "What shall I do now? My master is taking away my job. I'm not strong enough to dig, and I'm ashamed to beg—I know what I'll do so that, when I lose my job here, people will welcome me into their houses."

So he called in each one of his master's debtors. He asked the first, "How much do you owe my master?"

"Eight hundred gallons of olive oil," he replied.

The manager told him, "Take your bill, sit down quickly, and make it four hundred."

Then he asked the second, "And how much do you owe?"

"A thousand bushels of wheat," he replied.

He told him, "Take your bill and make it eight hundred."

The master commended the dishonest manager because he had acted shrewdly. For the people of this world are more shrewd in dealing with their own kind than are the people of the light. I tell you, use worldly wealth to gain friends for yourselves, so that when it is gone, you will be welcomed into eternal dwellings.

Whoever can be trusted with very little can also be trusted with much, and whoever is dishonest with very little will also be dishonest with much. So if you have not been trustworthy in handling worldly wealth, who will trust you with true riches? And if you have not been trustworthy with someone else's property, who will give you property of your own?

No servant can serve two masters. Either he will hate the one and love the other, or he will be devoted to the one and despise the other. You cannot serve both God and Money *(Luke 16:1-13).*

Here we are seen as stewards. We are not owners but are

in charge of his possessions. These goods are placed in our hands for a period of time, but ownership never transfers to us. What we do with the possessions (God's) is our focus.

It is at this point that the "new agenda" must be clear. It is not about money only. It is about all of life—all its gifts, possessions, and talents. If good and proper use of these benefits is to develop, there must be a relinquishment of ownership and possession. We must acknowledge that everything belongs to God, and we are put in charge to insure proper use of His gifts. Samuel Young said, "This idea of stewardship is also a vital issue in entering into the life of holiness by a full, personal consecration to God in the crisis of entire sanctification, and in the subsequent continuing life of holiness."[3]

This concept, then, for the Christian, focuses on God's creation. It encompasses all His gifts, including things, time, relationships, talents, money, earth, opportunities— to name a few. It is a person's response to His kindness. It recognizes responsibility for His world—being proactive in managing the gifts of the Creator. Thomas C. Rieke has written: "Each of us is a steward of a valuable but limited life. We are called to a holiness and a wholeness of living which acknowledges both beginning and ending."[4]

To realize that God shares His created goodness with us is mind-boggling. Ronald Vallet writes, "Why is God willing to share resources with us? Because God has chosen to call us and accept us as servants and stewards."[5] Paul states, "This is how one should regard us, as servants of Christ and stewards of the mysteries of God" (1 Cor. 4:1, RSV).

In her book *Time, Talents, Things,* Latayne C. Scott gives this summary of a steward: "The steward tries to manage the way the owner would manage; the steward cares for the household the way the master would care."[6] The responsibility of a steward is to act on behalf of the owner, or Creator.

It is this factor that must be understood. The Christian is a person under biblical mandate to act as the Creator would act, to respond to the opportunities of life as He would respond, and to handle life's treasures and talents as He would handle them. Thomas Rieke puts this in perspective when he writes, "To be a steward is to handle wisely the occasions which life presents to us. Far from being limited to the use of money, stewardship is so inclusive as to concern itself with attitudes and actions and alacrity."[7]

From these definitions one can see that stewardship is one's response to God's gifts. Without a strong belief that God is Creator, and an encompassing belief in the sovereignty of God, stewardship, in the biblical sense, is impossible. Without a strong belief in biblical creation, one is prone to take a stance of ownership that rules out a proper mind-set toward things.

There are two characteristics of a biblical steward that are basic. First, that which is entrusted to him—time, talent, treasure—does not belong to him but belongs to God. Second, he will be held accountable for that which is placed in his trust.

Out of these basic facts, two responses emerge—responsibility and accountability, which were addressed in chapter 2. The steward is responsible for proper use and is accountable both for proper use or abuse. In his book, *Stepping Stones of the Steward,* Ronald Vallet quotes an excellent summary of stewardship from John H. Westerhoff. It reads:

> Stewardship is nothing less than a complete life-style, a total accountability and responsibility before God. Stewardship is what we do after we say we believe, that is, after we give our love, loyalty, and trust to God, from whom each and every aspect of our lives comes as a gift. As members of God's household, we are subject to God's economy or stewardship, that is, God's plan to reconcile the whole world and bring creation to its proper end.[8]

The New Testament calls us to "be doers of the word, and not hearers only" (James 1:22, NKJV). James further reminds us that "anyone . . . who knows the good he ought to do and doesn't do it, sins" (4:17). The biblical perspective of stewardship is clear—each person has been given gifts of time, talent, and treasures. While not all are granted in equal measure, every person has some of each. We are stewards over whatever we have. God has entrusted us with these gifts and expects us to use them for His glory. Such living demands spiritual maturity and relinquishment. One must be more interested in caring for God's gifts than being owner of them. Eugene Peterson writes:

Christian spirituality means living in the mature wholeness of the gospel. It means taking all the elements of your life—children, spouse, job, weather, possessions, relationships—and experiencing them as an act of faith. God wants all the materials of our lives.[9]

Today's landscape is cluttered with the debris of selfish pursuits, the result of people thinking they owned the gifts God had given to them. From such misuse others have been deprived, and they themselves have been shortchanged. J. Kerby Anderson reminds us, "Mankind has abused every good gift God has given it, including nature, authority, sex, marriage, food and wealth."[10]

From creation God planned that people should enjoy His gifts, but under certain conditions. While God placed man in dominion over His creation, He gave parameters of responsibility and care. God has not changed those parameters. He is still Owner, Creator, and Lord of all. Wise is that person who recognizes His ownership and gives attention to careful and faithful stewardship.

A kind of stewardship so necessary in the contemporary world is the proper handling of our resources. Too often they are handled carelessly and without concern for others or for the future. A good steward knows that all the things of life are important. He handles them with care and with respect, knowing that someday they will pass to others.

Use the talents you possess. The woods would be silent if only the birds that sing the best would sing.

But seek first his kingdom and his righteousness, and all these things will be given to you as well *(Matt. 6:33)*.

Command those who are rich in this present world not to be arrogant nor to put their hope in wealth, which is so uncertain, but to put their hope in God, who richly provides us with everything for our enjoyment. Command them to do good, to be rich in good deeds, and to be generous and willing to share. In this way they will lay up treasure for themselves as a firm foundation for the coming age *(1 Tim. 6:17-19)*.

4

Time, Talent, and Things

Things

I found a clipping in a book that was passed along to me. It bore no documentation; however, its message was clear. It read:

> I had gone from college to Hollywood, where I was put under contract to a motion picture studio and promised a creative career. I thoroughly enjoyed my work . . . it was fun, exciting, and lucrative—and I loved the people! Materially, my background had been very simple, and for the first time in my life I had some of the things I always thought I wanted . . . plus glamorous surroundings, stimulating work, and talented people. Yet underneath the surface of my being—deep down in my spirit—my possessions added up to zero. I had more of everything, but "everything" was not enough. The gnawing hunger was still there.

"Everything was not enough." Things are not the answer. Life, as created by God, was designed for higher pursuits than the temporal and for greater purpose than accumulation of things. If there is one lesson here, it is that life is more than things.

The apostle Paul has some advice for us pertaining to possessions. He wrote:

> But whatever was to my profit I now consider loss for the sake of Christ. What is more, I consider everything a loss compared to the surpassing greatness of knowing Christ Jesus my Lord, for whose sake I have lost all things. I consider them rubbish, that I may gain Christ (Phil. 3:7-8).

Paul was not condemning possessions or things. He was putting them in perspective to life's purpose. Paul was writing about priority—the priority of keeping the Lordship of Christ over all things. Priority living is what stewardship is all about. For Paul, and for all Christians, putting Christ and His cause and His way first is primary. Jesus instructed us to "seek first his kingdom and his righteousness, and all these things will be given to you as well" (Matt. 6:33).

Priority affects possessions. A deep commitment to Christ gives proper value and place to possessions. Possessions and things are not wrong, in and of themselves. When our possessions are properly aligned to the Lordship of Christ, proper stewardship is taking place. Every possession must be weighed on the priority-value scale. Does it fit in God's plan? Will it help, or hinder, my doing God's will? Will it make life better spiritually, and not just better? To be better off—with possessions—is not necessarily to be better. Will possession distract, detour, or diminish my walk with the Lord? Will these possessions increase my effectiveness in Kingdom representation? Such are the questions of stewardship.

The danger lurking in regard to possessions is always one of attitude and allegiance. If one is properly grounded in Christ and in His Word, there is a safe and reliable response mechanism ready to evaluate any possession. One's allegiance to Christ keeps possessions in their proper place.

Where there is anemic commitment, or no commitment at all, the door is opened for possessions to determine priority and purpose. An old axiom declares, "Whatever gets our attention, gets us." Without a value base from which to order possessions, they invade life quietly, and it is not long before things possess the person rather than the person possessing things.

The message of authentic stewardship is that one must have a deep commitment to Christ, an understanding of His Word, and an obedient spirit.

We discuss possessions in terms not only of things but also of other facets to the picture. Time, talent, and treasures are a part of the responsibility entrusted to persons. These must meet the same priority test as things.

Time

Everyone has 24 hours a day. It does not matter how rich or poor one is, or how many academic degrees one has, each person is gifted with an equal amount of time. Time is given to us as a gift from God to use for His glory. Stewardship includes our proper use of time.

What are the priorities for the Christian in time planning? Purposes, values, character, mission are a few. In any workaday schedule there will be commitment to employment that involves the nitty-gritty things that must be done in the workplace. This consumes a large chunk of time for all of us and is necessary to "make a living."

Stewardship in the workplace will be covered in another chapter. Our interest here is to see time as a trust—a gift from God to be invested in a purpose and mission consistent with God's plan for our life.

The Bible has something to say about time. The Psalmist advises us, "Remember how short [our] time is" (89:47, NKJV). Ecclesiastes says, "There is a time for everything, and a season for every activity under heaven" (3:1). Paul encourages us to "understand . . . the present time" (Rom. 13:11). He further admonishes us to "walk circumspectly, not as fools but as wise, redeeming the time" (Eph. 5:15-16, NKJV).

The Christian lives with a consciousness of the importance of time. The Puritans, who so deeply influenced John Wesley, saw the events and opportunities of life as "God moments." Someone said, "They believed that there was never a moment when God was not present with them for guidance, comfort, and strength. The challenge of the spiritual life was to live with an increasing consciousness of this fact."[1]

"God moments," as perceived by the Puritans, were based on a deep understanding of time. Steve Harper points out that there are two Greek words for time, *chronos* and *kairos*. He states:

> *Chronos* time is the chronological, sequential passage of time. It includes seconds, minutes, hours, days. *Kairos* time is time within time. We could describe it as the presence and activity of God in the midst of our time. It is a quality in the midst of quantity. As Christians, we believe that our lives *(chronos)* can be lived as God's presence *(kairos)* fills and guides our actions.[2]

The good steward must see time as a "God moment" in which one has opportunity to invest one's talent and treasures. Time is a gift one cannot store, but that must not be wasted. Stewardship is about caring for the trust of time. William Arthur Ward states that "to waste time is irreverence to God."[3]

Some of the biggest stress factors in contemporary life are the time pressures. Where there is no priority scale, events, activities, and pursuits can overload the system. We are paying a big price for such stress overload. J. Grant Howard said, "The solution to our schizophrenic schedules is to establish the proper priorities. If we are going to get out of the rat race and live relaxed, normal lives, then we have to get our priorities straight."[4]

Prioritizing must be a process for the steward. Thomas Rieke states that "Christian stewards need to recapture a sense of the immense value of time. It is 'high' time—lofty and noble and worthwhile. It is not made for wasting but for offering opportunity. It is time seen as measurable pieces of eternity."[5]

Talents

Everyone has a gift or a talent, just as everyone has 24 hours in a day. God gifted each person in order that everyone will fit somewhere into the mosaic of life. By using our gifts or talents, we are fulfilled, we feel needed, and, more importantly, we bring glory to our Creator.

One of my first church visits after being elected district superintendent was to a church whose pastor I had not met. Because of his work he had been unable to attend the assembly. When I entered the church, I greeted a fine gentleman and inquired if he might be the pastor. "No," he said, "I'm just a greeter." I encouraged the gentleman by reminding him that he certainly was not "just" a greeter. I pointed out he was the most important person any visitor would meet, for he would, in a large way, determine whether they ever came back. He was a good example of a person using his talent in the mosaic of the church.

God intended that His gifts be used in good and proper ways. Where they are not used, or are misused, there is disruption and dissatisfaction.

There are four things to remember about the stewardship of talents:

1. Each is given by God, for good use.
2. Each is given, not to fulfill self, but to help others.
3. We are responsible for the use of the gift, not the responses to the gift.
4. We will give an account for the use of our talents.

"Part of our responsibility as stewards," wrote Latayne C. Scott, "is to recognize what abilities God has given us and then be willing to use those abilities for His purposes."[6] Paul wrote: "There are different kinds of gifts, but the same Spirit. There are different kinds of service, but the same Lord. There are different kinds of working, but the same God works all of them in all men" (1 Cor. 12:4-6).

No two individuals may be gifted in the same way. Some will be multi-gifted, while others may struggle to find one gift. But each of us is gifted, and we are to use our gift to build the Body of Christ. Paul continues, "all these [talents/gifts] are the work of one and the same Spirit, and he gives them to each one, just as he determines" (v. 11).

Paul elaborates on the wide use of gifts by declaring, "The body is a unit, though it is made up of many parts;

and though all its parts are many, they form one body. . . .
Now the body is not made up of one part but of many"
(vv. 12, 14). We are stewards in concert, as we blend our
talents with others to serve and strengthen the church.

One cannot discuss talents without looking at the
Lord's discourse on talents and accountability in Matthew
25. Several things stand out in this passage:

1. Talents are given as a trust—"[He] entrusted his
   property to them" (v. 14).
2. Talents are determined by the Master—"To one he
   gave five talents . . . , to another two talents, and to
   another one talent" (v. 15). See 1 Cor. 12:11.
3. Each is accountable for his own talents—"After a
   long time the master of those servants returned and
   settled accounts with them" (v. 19).
4. God is pleased with talents that are put to work—
   "The man who had received the five talents brought
   the other five. 'Master,' he said, 'you entrusted me
   with five talents. See, I have gained five more.'

   "His master replied, 'Well done, good and faithful
   servant! You have been faithful with a few things; I
   will put you in charge of many things. Come and
   share your master's happiness!'" (vv. 20-21, see 22-23).
5. God will judge those who do not use their talents—
   "Then the man who had received the one talent
   came. 'Master,' he said, 'I knew that you are a hard
   man, harvesting where you have not sown and
   gathering where you have not scattered seed. So I
   was afraid and went out and hid your talent in the
   ground. See, here is what belongs to you.'

   "His master replied, 'You wicked, lazy servant!
   So you knew that I harvest where I have not sown
   and gather where I have not scattered seed? Well
   then, you should have put my money on deposit
   with the bankers, so that when I returned I would
   have received it back with interest.

"'Take the talent from him and give it to the one who has the ten talents. For everyone who has will be given more, and he will have an abundance. Whoever does not have, even what he has will be taken from him. And throw that worthless servant outside, into the darkness, where there will be weeping and gnashing of teeth'" (vv. 24-30).

It is interesting that the Lord had most to say to the person who had hid his talent. What this parable teaches is summarized by Thomas Wolfe, who wrote:

If a man has a talent and cannot use it, he has failed. If he has a talent and uses only half of it, he has partly failed. If he has a talent and learns somehow to use the whole of it, he has gloriously succeeded and won a satisfaction and a triumph few men ever know.[7]

Find the person who has been a good steward of his possessions, his world, his opportunities, and you will find a person with meaningful purpose throbbing in his life. Stewardship is partnership with God.

Stewardship involves all of life, its talents, time, and treasure. Wise is that person who realizes the importance of all areas.

Remember this: Whoever sows sparingly will also reap sparingly, and whoever sows generously will also reap generously. Each man should give what he has decided in his heart to give, not reluctantly or under compulsion, for God loves a cheerful giver *(2 Cor. 9:6-7)*.

But store up for yourselves treasures in heaven, where moth and rust do not destroy, and where thieves do not break in and steal. For where your treasure is, there your heart will be also *(Matt. 6:20-21)*.

5

What Does Stewardship Have to Do with Money?

When one talks of stewardship, the word that comes to mind most often is money. Someone has suggested, "Maybe money is the only thing we've ever given to the Lord—that's why we equate it with stewardship." But there is more to it than money. R. T. Williams reminded us, "Stewardship is taking a right attitude toward things and forming proper relationship with things."[1] That is what this chapter is all about.

What we hear concerning the subject is usually related to money. Most fund-raising campaigns tie this emphasis into their appeal. Unfortunately, stewardship is seldom used in church communication unless it relates to budgets or buildings, both of which involve money. It is true that it covers money, just as it covers all areas of life. We are stewards of money; in truth, probably more than in anything else it is a thermometer of whether our commitment is adequate. So a discussion of stewardship and money is important. Unless we come to a right view and use of money, everything else in this area is out of perspective.

There are two dangers in the area of money, as it relates to stewardship. One is to see the whole thing only as a money matter. This ignores the broader areas of responsibility and renders stewardship null and void in the long view. It excuses one from the wider responsibilities of life. This myopic perspective is neither good stewardship nor good giving. It ignores a major principle of the New Testament and fails to relate to the needs of others or to a life-encompassing principle.

Every pastor and church board member could recall someone who has said, "I'll pay the bill if someone else will do the work." Sometimes the better stewardship—consistent with purpose and long-range commitment—is to be part of the work force rather than giving the money. Most pastors are aware that genuine Christianity must go beyond the pocketbook. It must reach the heart. When it is a heart issue, and not just a money issue, it has greater impact for all involved.

The Christian community needs a revival of serving and sharing. It needs to see stewardship stretching its meaning into all areas of life, fulfilling those who extend and helping those to whom it is extended. Dr. Richard Lee Spindle wrote:

> There is a new freedom in living and serving and giving. Too many of us have gotten comfortable and have forgotten the joy of serving. It all flows out of digging, lifting, and extending, and not out of grabbing or getting or accumulating.[2]

The second danger in regards to money is that where money is seen as the end game, the individual misses out on the positive benefits of a wider approach. The other areas of life are untouched, then, if money is the only thing touched by one's view of accountability. It leaves everything else open to humanistic accounting and selfish disposal.

The individual stands to be the greatest loser in this misappropriation of responsibility. The things he adds to life, or subtracts, flow through channels unchecked by a proper principle. There is no ultimate purpose that governs the desire. The eventual product is a selfish person whose world is untouched by a responsible way of looking at things.

The individual is not the only loser in this misappropriation. Those around him suffer from the unbalanced philosophy. The needs and concerns of surrounding persons go unheeded and unmet, at least by him. Too often he tosses money at the needs, feeling he has done his part. Bertrand Russell said, "It is preoccupation with possession, more than anything else, that prevents men from living freely and nobly."[3]

Certainly the church suffers from a stewardship that is only money-focused. While churches always seem to need money, we must not conclude that is all they need. Too many are deceived into thinking that giving money is somehow the sum total of stewardship. In fact, one could gather from some television hoopla that money is all God is interested in, and if one just gives enough, his or her soul will be saved, and everything else will be taken care of. It is a great injustice to the concept of stewardship and to the souls of people. We owe people the challenge of the gospel, which is to a total commitment of life. We shortchange them where we preach less. I don't suggest that we do away with the offering or the pledge campaign. Giving is God's way of building His church and His people. But I do suggest that stewardship is more than giving. It is a total view of life that sees everything under the authority of God.

Stewardship that sees everything under the category of responsible care not only will make giving by tithes and offerings a priority but also will give other things as well, such as time and talents. What all of this brings us to is the meaning of life. What is our purpose? For what were we created? It is something too seldom considered in discussions. Alexander Solzhenitsyn wrote these words from a Soviet prison: "The meaning of earthly existence is not as we have grown used to thinking, in prosperity, but in the development of the soul."[4]

The basic question is, "What is it that belongs to God?" The answer, as we have seen, is *everything*. Richard Austin Thompson concluded that:

> If "the earth is the Lord's . . ." then it will affect our attitude toward all that we call our belongings. Our notion of ownership itself will change as we awaken to how we are but stewards, trustees of everything—from our institutions of government to our use of land and water; from houses to which we hold title to the persons whom we call family.[5]

Stewardship, as we have noted, has to do with responsibility and accountability. We are responsible to handle the treasures God has given us in a right and honorable manner, and accountability is the final proof of the way stewardship was implemented. In no area of life is this more meaningful than when it pertains to life's treasures.

Our response to treasures—how we handle them—tells much about the rest of our lives. Look at a person's checkbook, and you can quickly determine his or her priorities. Jesus said, "For where your treasure is, there your heart will be also" (Matt. 6:21).

It is sometimes hard for us to acknowledge the Bible's message about treasures, especially money. It's as if we think money is a 20th-century idea and these writers knew nothing about it. Our Lord Jesus Christ, who knows the potential of people and their propensity toward the material, had more to say about money than about most other subjects. This comes as a surprise to a lot of people, like the man who said to his pastor after a message on tithing, "What does money have to do with the gospel?" Quite a bit, for what we do with our possessions is a window on the soul. It reveals priorities and commitment.

Here is a sampling of what the Bible says about treasures and money:

> Do not store up for yourselves treasures on earth, where moth and rust destroy, and where thieves break in

and steal. But store up for yourselves treasures in heaven, where moth and rust do not destroy, and where thieves do not break in and steal. For where your treasure is, there your heart will be also *(Matt. 6:19-21).*

But godliness with contentment is great gain. For we brought nothing into the world, and we can take nothing out of it. But if we have food and clothing, we will be content with that. People who want to get rich fall into temptation and a trap and into many foolish and harmful desires that plunge men into ruin and destruction. For the love of money is a root of all kinds of evil. Some people, eager for money, have wandered from the faith and pierced themselves with many griefs *(1 Tim. 6:6-10).*

Other pertinent passages include Matt. 25:14-30, the parable of the talents, and Luke 19:11-27, the parable of the pounds (see RSV).

Out of the biblical message on money and treasures, these conclusions are offered:

1. All our treasures, including money, belong to God—not just 10 percent, or the tithe, but all of them. God does not say anywhere that I am steward of 10 percent. He says I am steward of *all* that He has loaned me. God retains ownership. He simply loans to you and me all we have, be it talents, treasures, time, family, friends, jobs—the list is endless. Latayne C. Scott has reminded us of this so simply: "What we don't readily understand is that when God gives us time, talents, and things, they still belong to Him. He doesn't give up His ownership."[6]

2. Tithing is a biblical principle. God knew something about humankind's thirst for ownership. Sin makes a man selfish. Sin blinds a person to the needs of others and, most of all, to the ways and will of God.

Consider these biblical teachings on the tithe and giving:

"Will a man rob God? Yet you rob me. But you ask, 'How do we rob you?' In tithes and offerings. You are under a curse—the whole nation of you—because you are robbing me. Bring the whole tithe into the storehouse, that there may be food in my house. Test me in this," says the Lord Almighty, "and see if I will not throw open the floodgates of heaven and pour out so much blessing that you will not have room enough for it" (Mal. 3:8-10).

A tithe of everything from the land, whether grain from the soil or fruit from the trees, belongs to the Lord; it is holy to the Lord (Lev. 27:30).

The Lord said to Moses, "Speak to the Levites and say to them: 'When you receive from the Israelites the tithe I give you as your inheritance, you must present a tenth of that tithe as the Lord's offering'" (Num. 18:25-26).

Give, and it will be given to you. A good measure, pressed down, shaken together and running over, will be poured into your lap. For with the measure you use, it will be measured to you (Luke 6:38).

Freely you have received, freely give (Matt. 10:8).

It is more blessed to give than to receive (Acts 20:35).

Whoever can be trusted with very little can also be trusted with much, and whosoever is dishonest with very little will also be dishonest with much. So if you have not been trustworthy in handling worldly wealth, who will trust you with true riches? And if you have not been trustworthy with someone else's property, who will give you property of your own? (Luke 16:10-12).

But just as you excel in everything—in faith, in speech, in knowledge, in complete earnestness and in your love for us—see that you also excel in this grace of giving (2 Cor. 8:7).

God, in His command to tithe, is asking us to include Him in our financial planning. Our journey with Him is an opportunity for us to express His Lordship over everything.

Moreover, tithing does something for us. By the giving of tithes I have relinquished "first rights" to God. I have acknowledged Him as Lord and have committed myself to trust Him. Giving is one way God uses to grow His people. Donald Krabill has reminded us that "the unfortunate problem with tithing is that it focuses our attention on how much we give rather than on how much we keep. God doesn't care much about what we give. He's primarily concerned about what we hang on to."[7]

We need to understand, however, that our tithing does not obligate God to bless us. Our blessings come from His love and grace, not because of what we do or do not do. This is the part of God that the wealth-and-health preachers and writers have not understood. Their giving is based on selfishness. If one gives enough, their thinking goes, then He is obligated to bless. Such giving is motivated by the desire to get something. The premise of giving, then, rests with what the person does. God is in neutral, just waiting for the giving to trigger His response. Love and grace, His key characteristics, are ignored in the equation.

The wealth-and-health philosophy is destructive for at least two reasons. First, it misuses the goodness of God. His nature is to give, to bless, to love. Many times, due to the wealth-and-health equation, such responses from Him are interpreted as responses to giving. He is seen as a bookkeeper who balances the books and must recognize when someone has given a "seed faith" gift. This robs Him of sovereign freedom to bless as divine wisdom chooses, out of a heart of love and grace.

Second, the wealth-and-health mentality teaches people to use God. It encourages people to turn to Him when there is a need, or a crisis, and to bargain for His help through giving. The biblical message is that we cannot earn our way into His grace, for it is a gift and is available to every person.

Tithing, then, is not our bargaining chip with God. It is the expression of our love and trust, an acknowledgment that He is Lord.

This chapter has dealt with treasures, money, tithing—loaded words in contemporary vocabulary. This is the side of life's ledger that can so easily be confused. Treasures and money seem to have a way of changing people for the worse, often, rather than the better. Money can give a false security, tempting a person to rely on such security rather than spiritual things. Henri Nouwen wrote, "Wealth takes away sharp edges of our moral sensitivities and allows a comfortable confusion about sin and virtue."[8]

Stewardship asks us to review our agendas. It asks for radical changes in accountability where the things of God are being misused or ignored. It asks us to shift the emphasis from getting to giving, from accumulation to accountability, and from what we give to why we give. God wants us to use and enjoy His gifts, but He knows this will only happen where He retains ownership. William Wells said, "In Eden, wealth obviously had little to do with bank accounts. The point was not accumulation, but enjoyment and proper use of the creation God had provided."[9] This is still the correct agenda.

Stewardship takes the talents and treasures of life, however many there are, and multiplies them through sharing and serving. The wise steward is not one who counts his talents or gifts, but one who makes opportunities count by using what he has in a good and useful way.

Where there is no stewardship in life, there great opportunities are passed by, exciting causes are missed, and an emptiness comes where meaning might have been.

Then the eleven disciples went to Galilee, to the mountain where Jesus had told them to go. When they saw him, they worshiped him; but some doubted. Then Jesus came to them and said, "All authority in heaven and on earth has been given to me. Therefore go and make disciples of all nations, baptizing them in the name of the Father and of the Son and of the Holy Spirit, and teaching them to obey everything I have commanded you. And surely I will be with you always, to the very end of the age" *(Matt. 28:16-20)*.

Jesus said to him, "Today salvation has come to this house, because this man, too, is a son of Abraham. For the Son of Man came to seek and to save what was lost" *(Luke 19:9-10)*.

6

Stewardship Revisits the Church

Is there any new word about stewardship for the Church? I would not be so presumptuous as to say so. What I would propose is that something new and profound is not needed. What we do need is a recasting of the basics. Probably no area in the Church needs a return to the basics like this area. That, in itself, would be a new agenda for some.

The Church needs to hear again that stewardship is more than money. The church that feels its stewardship base is covered when it has raised money and completed its pledge campaign is neglectful and wanting in its teaching.

The first question of stewardship, for the Church, is about mission. God's Church is called into existence to make a difference in a sinful and rebellious world. To accomplish this, the Church must be steward of what He has given to fulfill its mission. He equips His Church to do His mission. But our first task is to be faithful stewards of what He has given!

To address our mission, we must develop an attitude that sees everything as a gift from God. Just as individuals are stewards of His gifts, so is the Church. Thus, buildings, people, opportunities, prospects, needs, money—all are a part of the stewardship factor.

The Church, by and large, is a great institution. It is doing more than most on a variety of fronts to address the needs and hurts of the world. In a few isolated instances the Church may be wanting, but its overall track record far exceeds any that would be in second place.

The primary challenge facing the Church is to keep addressing the crucial issues, lest the temptation to greed and glory take it away from its mission. George Barna, in his perceptive book *The Frog in the Kettle*, writes this:

> America in the 90's is rotting from the inside out. We are suffering from constant, if almost imperceptible, shifts in perspective and behavior. As our population matures in technological sophistication and material comfort, we are losing our spiritual edge. We have embraced the means rather than the ends. Service to God has been replaced by a thirst for exaltation of self.[1]

Bill Hull, in his book *The Disciple-Making Pastor*, makes the point that "the people in the pew ask all the wrong questions, based on cultural programming: What can the church do for me? Can I get my needs met here? Do I feel good when I leave here? Does the pastor make me feel guilty? Will I have to do what I don't feel like doing?"[2] Later, Hull diagnoses the questions by saying, "These questions and more reflect the corruption of self-idolatry primarily fostered in our society by the secular psychological community."[3]

Hull identifies the self-idolatry problem as a

> development of a "need theology" that finds its roots in gratifying the desires of the flesh. Therefore, the most popular theologies of today are directed toward immediate need gratification. Television lends itself perfectly to the message, which is often called the healthy-wealthy heresy.[4]

Good stewardship constantly requires that the Church keep its mission and purpose clear. The Church should be first, and always, the voice of God and of righteousness in a sinful world. When our mission is neglected, people and needs are unattended, and no deterrent to sin is in place. Hull observes, "The superficial Christian wants to have all the benefits of a victorious Christian life without the commitment."[5] Stewardship is a commitment to the biblical mandate to take care of God's resources in ways that bring glory to Him.

The Church must ever be aware that the materialism of the world has invaded the pew. Author Stephen Eyre has put it more boldly: "The dragon of materialism has moved into the church in blatant ways. Many Christians believe that God's blessings mean material prosperity for all who ask for them. The gospel, behind the flame of this dragon, becomes the gospel of prosperity."[6]

One of the big tasks of the church is to guard its mission from the encroachment of this "dragon of materialism." Another has written, "For men and women with mission, freedom is rejecting the entanglement of possessive influences so they are able to speak, move, and think in life with their life's purpose."[7]

Faithfulness to mission implies that money will be a factor in the stewardship equation, but a factor of service rather than of selfishness. It is not by accident that growing churches are sharing and giving churches. Those leading such churches have read the pages of the New Testament and have discovered that giving to others is a signal of obedience to mission. Because they know the biblical model of the Church well, they give rightly.

Some churches do not "give to get." They have not been sucked into the wealth-and-health syndrome, nor do they hold God hostage through their giving by dictating what He returns to them. They simply see the fulfillment of mission as priority and proper stewardship.

Unless the Church sees its purpose and mission in partnership with God and His plan to reach the world, it will become self-centered and chart a record of inadequate stewardship. Ronald Vallet writes, "Failure to see the ministry of the church as participating in God's mission makes it difficult for churches and individuals to participate fully in the purpose of God."[8]

God has entrusted a great mission to His Church—a

mission to make disciples everywhere. He has gifted His Church to fulfill that mission. The church that does not see itself as steward of His gifts, and feel the compulsion to be an honorable one, is wanting in the Christian arena. Such a church is a candidate for decline, disappointment, and disunity.

Stewardship calls the Church to give more attention to mission, to evangelism, to prayer, to outreach, than to money matters. Where a church is mission-driven, there a philosophy and purpose in regards to money is lifted above the inward and selfish and is seen as stewardship to the glory of God.

Churches, then, have two options. They can be mission-driven and open themselves to the needs around them, or they can be inward-conscious, serving themselves at the expense of others. Richard Halverson wrote, "Man was meant to be a channel, not a reservoir. When man shuts up the outgo in his life, he stagnates. His life gets clogged. When he lets go, opens the channel, he mellows and matures."[9] It is so for the Church as well.

A few years ago I was called to discuss finances with one of the churches on our district. They were behind several thousand dollars in bills, including their mortgage and budgets. As we discussed the financial crisis, I felt I had exhausted all possibilities in my effort to help them. We had pruned the budget to bare bones and were at an impasse. Finally, I asked the board when they felt the crisis started. Could they point to a problem? Did some top givers move away? It was all strange, because attendance was up rather dramatically.

Several gave suggestions or reasons why they thought finances were down, and why and when it started. None really made sense. Finally, a little old lady in tennis shoes spoke for the first time in the meeting. Through tears she said, "I can tell you when our financial troubles started. It was about six years ago when we voted to stop paying budgets. From that time on, we have struggled. My husband, now deceased, and I begged the board not to do it."

The church has the same responsibility of stewardship that a Christian does. It must see all of its ministry and gifts, opportunities and facilities, money and people, as that over which they are trustees with eternal accountability.

Stewardship responsibilities stretch a church beyond its four walls, to responsible and compassionate involvement in the community, addressing the social, political, economic, and cultural issues as the people of God. Stewardship, for the church, is a call to minister to those whom God brings into its fellowship. Every prospect, then, is an opportunity—a responsibility—of stewardship. It is an opportunity to share the gospel, to minister to needs, to draw people into the life of the church and its mission. It is an opportunity for the people of God to share its message, its mission, and its Master.

Stewardship, then, calls the Church to faithfulness—faithfulness to the Word of God, to theological truths, to mission, to spiritual nurture and discipleship, and to financial accountability. To accomplish such an all-encompassing task means that the Church must be a good steward of the spiritual gifts God plants within the body of believers. C. Peter Wagner reminds us: "Every spiritual gift we have is a resource that we must use and for which we will be held accountable at the judgment."[10]

Recently I read Allan Cox's book, *Straight Talk for Monday Morning*. In one chapter he referred to a businessman who was concerned about the "ethics of performance." Cox wrote that "he simply cares about the stewardship of his business."[11] he went on to conclude that "he knows the health of any enterprise is based not on what we take but on what we give."[12]

Earlier Cox alluded to Harvard Business School's

problem of incorporating ethics into its curriculum. He asks, "Now why does Harvard's faculty have such a hard time figuring that out?" Then Cox writes, "Giving is the ultimate return on assets."[13]

It is interesting that the business world sometimes sees things that the Church does not. If "giving is the ultimate return on assets," then the Church must survey its stewardship and review its "ethics of performance" to see if mission still has priority.

The Church is at its best when it is proclaiming and modeling love, forgiveness, hope, and understanding. When it gets sidetracked from these proclamations, then it ceases to be the Church God envisioned and commissioned.

The Church serves best when it serves unselfishly, with intent to share rather than receive.

May the favor of the Lord our God rest upon us; establish the work of our hands for us—yes, establish the work of our hands *(Ps. 90:17).*

The man who plants and the man who waters have one purpose, and each will be rewarded according to his own labor. For we are God's fellow workers; you are God's field, God's building *(1 Cor. 3:8-9).*

7

The Stewardship of Work

From the beginning of time work has been part of the human story. The Genesis account reads, "The Lord God took the man and put him in the Garden of Eden to work it and take care of it" (2:15). Soon thereafter, due to the sin of Adam and Eve, God said to Adam: "Cursed is the ground because of you; through painful toil you will eat of it all the days of your life" (Gen. 3:17).

The Bible has many references to work—Gen. 31:42; Exod. 20:9; Deut. 26:7; Neh. 4:6; Pss. 90:17; 104:23; 128:1-2; Eccles. 4:8-9; 8:9, NKJV; John 6:27; 17:4; 1 Cor. 3:8-9; 1 Thess. 5:12-13. Two things stand out in these references: one, our work should have purpose; two, our work is to glorify God.

Good stewardship demands that we examine our work in light of the following questions: "What is the purpose of our work?" "Where does stewardship enter the picture?" "In what ways am I steward of my work?"

Dennis Haack writes, "Faithfulness in work means consciously approaching work as part of God's good creation for us."[1] He says also that "faithfulness in work means that our work, regardless of its vocation, is to be rendered as obedient, spiritual service to God."[2]

For many caught in the workaday whirl where drudgery and pressure are the order of the day, it is difficult to see any connection with stewardship. It is here that humans in the near 21st century feel the effects of man's fall in the Garden of Eden. Haack explains: "The Fall didn't remove the significance of our work, but it did twist work into something different from what God intended."[3]

People in today's world need to reference their work dilemmas to creation and the Fall. Haack wrote, "Working in a fallen world means constantly leaning against the effects of the Fall. Just as we pull weeds in a garden, so we must labor to increasingly bring Shalom to every aspect of creation that is under the curse of sin, including the workplace."[4]

Admittedly, this can be small comfort to the person whose job is demeaning and even sheer torture. But the challenge of stewardship is to see purpose in the workplace and be steward of its opportunity or its misery. Leland Ryken asserted, "The early Puritans saw their shop as well as their chapel as holy ground."[5]

For the Christian, work is no more pleasant, at times, than it is for the non-Christian. This is true for those in ministry, at whatever level. What is operating in the arena of work, for the Christian, is a basic responsibility to be steward of all life's opportunities and moments. It means to see work as a way to invest life, not make a living. Darius Salter wrote these meaningful words: "God's master purpose for the Christian is not occupational employment but fulfilling a day-to-day moment-by-moment mission of the Holy Spirit."[6]

When people find mission and purpose even in the lowest of tasks, they can endure any circumstance. It is true, even in the most tedious of jobs, that happiness is not dependent on circumstances. Stewardship asks the worker to place one's work in a broader perspective. Every Christian is on a mission to live out, in a redemptive way, the moments God has given. In the workplace, we are stewards of our time as well as opportunity to lay claim to the strength and grace of Christ. Haack wrote, "Every legitimate vocation and trade pursued as service to God is part of the spiritual task of pushing back the Fall."[7]

Work, then, for the Christian is more than just making a living—it is making a life. Eternal priorities set the drudgery of the workplace in a better perspective. It may not mean the work is more attractive, the atmosphere more pleasant, or the stress and pressure any less intimidating. But, it could mean that the ability to endure now has the support and strength of a purpose that reaches beyond the job. It is this that gives dignity to work.

The big question that plagues a multitude of workers is, "How can I make any sense of this job?" In an earthly sense, there may be no satisfying answer. But to be steward of the workplace, even in the humblest and smallest of ways, is to give dignity to work.

I knew a man who worked at what others would probably consider the lowest of jobs. However, his dependability was an inspiration to his employer and his joyful spirit an inspiration to those with whom he worked. In the community he was known as a man who cared deeply and shared graciously. When he retired, his boss said of him, "He was a man who made all of us feel better. He made life appealing!"

The task for the Christian is to make the job fit into the larger mosaic of life. For most, the job consumes a larger part of time than any other task, and it must be part of life's greater purpose if it is to give dignity to existence. One part of the mosaic for Christians is that we witness, even on the job, to redemptive realities. Thus the workplace is a place of witness. One's life is on display for those hours, and others are taking a reading on attitude, priorities, integrity, honesty, and faithfulness.

To go from the work arena with a silent, or even spoken, witness about Him who makes life endurable in both the crucial and the drudging times is fulfillment of the responsibility of stewardship. Steve Harper reminds us that "the greatest hope we have for the influencing of society is as we connect our faith to our vocations and move out into the world to live as committed Christians."[8] Our faith must be expressed in and through our work if our lives make any impact for the glory of God.

Paul wrote that we are "God's fellow workers" (2 Cor. 6:1). While it is easy, and common, for us to interpret this in a spiritual context, we must also take this verse into the workplace. We must lift our work, whatever it is, to the level of partnership with God and be encouraged by the fact that He is with us in our tasks.

Stewardship in relation to work begins with the purpose of our Christian life rather than with the job. Our Christian commitment should define the job rather than the job defining our existence. Harper states:

> We desperately need to understand that the fundamental definition of our life is CHRISTIAN. Too often we define ourselves by what we do . . . But function never defines our personhood. Instead, we are defined by who we are. Once this idea really captures us, we will begin to be the agents of witness and renewal which our Lord intends for us to be.[9]

The task of stewardship is to guard against the invasion of the secular. The workplace, because it often seems so far removed from anything Christian, can chip away at our self-image and make us feel less than Christian. We must remember that we are not defined by our work but defined by our commitments and faith. Eugene Peterson cautioned, "If I, even for a moment, accept my culture's definition of me, I am rendered harmless."[10]

Richard Winwood has said:

> People who are in control in their personal lives will more likely be in control in their business (or work) lives as well. Our lives are, in fact, not segmented into nice parcels of work, home, family, community, etc. But are part of an integrated whole. Instability in one area will unavoidably affect the other areas as well.[11]

Work is a privilege, though some debate this at times. It is one way we bring dignity to our being. Earl Palmer, in his book, *Signposts*, writes:

The good result of work, in addition to the task completed, is that through hard work we are enabled to develop our full stride as human beings. It is through work that a young man or woman develops the skills and talents of his or her particular uniqueness. Both rest and work help us to feel good about ourselves, not only about what we think and feel, but also about what we do and what we can make.[12]

A proper view of work is to have come to terms with life's eternal purpose and then fit that purpose into our work. Only then is there an integrated meaning to all of life, which touches the workplace with dignity and fulfillment.

Work provides the opportunity for life to contribute to some cause, however small it might be. It is when life loses sight of its cause that living becomes drudgery.

Work is a good discipline. Where such a discipline is learned, it serves to keep life on course, pursuing its goal.

But seek first his kingdom and his righteousness, and all these things will be given to you as well. Therefore do not worry about tomorrow, for tomorrow will worry about itself. Each day has enough trouble of its own *(Matt. 6:33-34).*

But whatever was to my profit I now consider loss for the sake of Christ. What is more, I consider everything a loss compared to the surpassing greatness of knowing Christ Jesus my Lord, for whose sake I have lost all things. I consider them rubbish, that I may gain Christ *(Phil. 3:7-8).*

8

The Stewardship of Success and Failure

Success is a powerful word. For many it is the measurement of life. Somehow, everything else will fall into place if one can be successful. Such thinking is secular, and its untruth has been discovered by thousands who reach the land of success, only to find the fruit bitter and disappointing. But that is not the last word on success. One can be successful and enjoy the fruits thereof. Proper stewardship is the key.

Success, for the Christian, is not determined by position, things, or power, but by purpose, being, and service. Mother Teresa perhaps said it best: "God has not called me to be successful; He has called me to be faithful."

Success, for the Christian, is faithful stewardship of talents, things, opportunities, relationships—all of life. Where one has orchestrated these gifts through obedience to the will of God, success is the summary.

R. T. Williams, an early general superintendent in the Church of the Nazarene, wrote, "Success or failure depends upon one's ability and willingness to distinguish between the things that are important and the things that are not, or to properly relate values and emphasize them."[1] Success is a moving target. What one calls success at one stage in life changes through maturation and growth. It is important, therefore, that good stewardship is the basis of one's interpretation of success—stewardship that sees all of life as investment potential for God.

A decade ago, Czeslaw Milosz, professor of Slavic literature at the University of California at Berkeley, gave a lecture titled "The Erosion of Faith in America." Among other things, he said, "Men and women in Western culture have become self-referential." Earl Palmer, commenting about the lecture, wrote: "He explained that we live in a post-Christian era in which the old values that underpinned Western civilization are being replaced by individualized values that have their origin in the self."[2]

The "self-referential" philosophy is what a new agenda for stewardship addresses. Proper stewardship cannot operate with an equation of one. Thomas Rieke has reminded us, "We are not self-owners but newly freed slaves. Our liberty is not to be used selfishly but within the boundaries of the freedom which comes to God's children."[3]

While pastoring in Racine, Wis, I had preached a sermon on the surrendered life. A lady came to me and said surrender did not mean what I was trying to convey. She explained that her father had served in the army of a country overrun by enemy tanks and forced to surrender their arms. She said, "My father had to surrender on the outside, but on the inside he was still true to his country." I saw what she meant. Surrender could imply compliance, but with some reservation.

Our commitment to Christ is a commitment to His way, to His truth, to His purpose and plan for our lives. For such a commitment to be fulfilled, and growing, we must be constantly relinquishing our will to the highest and to the best. Linda and Richard Eyre wrote a book, Life Balance, in which they stated: "Too often we measure (and are measured) by position, title, income, appearance, credentials, contacts. It's easy to forget (or never look for) things like character, beliefs, integrity, commitment."[4]

Success for the Christian is seeking to know the whole will of God for all of life. We cannot compartmentalize our search. One cannot seek God's will for career but ignore

His will in other areas of life. Proper stewardship implies that there is balance, where all of life comes under the authority and wisdom of God. Dennis Haack writes, "The real struggle in life is not between success or failure as they are commonly understood. Rather, what should really grip our minds and hearts and imaginations is the challenge of pleasing God by being faithful across the full scope of our lives."[5]

The challenge of pleasing and serving God is the measure of success for the Christian. I had a talented pastor come to our district to lead a much smaller church than his previous assignment. Several asked him why he would do that. "Why step down?" they asked. I liked his reply: "In the will of God there is no size." Proper accountability asks, "What is God's will for me now?" Haack reminds us, "The world's measure of success must never be seen as the essence of life, because goodness is not defined by them."[6]

For the Christian, the quest for success begins with being, not power. As a new creation in Christ, the believer seeks first to be fashioned as the person Christ wants him or her to be. Out of this one's spiritual being the child of God seeks to be Christ's steward wherever challenge and opportunity knock. Haack gives us this reminder:

We will be held accountable for our response to God's blessings. Our Lord's standards are very high and consist of nothing less than his own holiness. Life is lived under the steady watchfulness of the God who is there . . . Someday, we will have to answer for our choices, our priorities and our values. They had better be informed by more rigorous stuff than the passing measures of modern success.[7]

Henri Nouwen has shared his journey of searching for the will of God. In his book *In the Name of Jesus*, he writes: "God is a God of the present and reveals to those who are willing to listen carefully to the moment . . . the steps they are to take in the future."[8] The Christian gives heed to the Lord's admonition, "But seek first his kingdom and his righteousness, and all these things will be given to you as well" (Matt. 6:33). All that falls within the parameters of His will is success. All that falls outside is the danger zone for a committed life. Nouwen relates an experience of searching for the will of God. "Everyone was saying that I was doing really well, but something inside was telling me that my success was putting my soul in danger."[9]

Authentic stewardship is the stance of the soul that can determine where the danger zones are and what makes for proper success. Haack encourages us: "Either we are living transformed lives or lives that are molded by the world. Conformity to the pattern of the world can hardly be the mark of success for a child of God."[10]

The successful Christian is the one who has found a way to embrace opportunities and enfold them into the will of God. Success for such a person is not the priority. The first choice is to do the will of God, and then to integrate appropriate opportunities into that will. Such a person will not let success become the thing that determines decisions or responses in life. The successful Christian is one who sees the challenges and opportunities as ways to make a living while, at the same time, making a life. But such making of a life, and doing the will of God, is the drumbeat.

In such a life, commitment to God governs proper responses and choices. As Christians, we view talents and things, opportunities and challenges, as gifts from Him to be handled carefully, wisely, and with prayer. All of this because accountability is a part of our involvement. Accountability is a discipline too often shunned by people, some even in the Christian ranks. But we know that, eventually, we will give an account to God for the things, opportunities, and talents entrusted to our care.

How Does a Steward Handle Failure?

A proper discussion of this subject must address failure.

How does the Christian handle failure? Are we stewards even of unsuccessful ventures?

The greatest efforts, the most dedicated attempts, sometimes wind up as failure. Alex MacKenzie wrote a book, *Time for Success*, in which he stated, "Success is doing your best."[11] Few will settle for this. We Christians can face failure if we have assurance that we have done our best. Granted, that may be small comfort when we face all the questions and fears related to failure. But the ultimate failure is failure to do the will of God. It is a truth that all of us need to hear.

There is one phrase that I use often in talking with pastors and their mates who are facing rejection, going through a crisis, or experiencing failure. It is that no church or person is the last—or first—word on their ministry. If we can pillow our heads at night knowing we have given God and the church our best, then God's word is "Well done," and that is an authentic and encouraging word for what appears to be failure. At the deep moment of failure we need to hear God's word and encouragement before we bring closure to the experience.

Sometimes the success syndrome towers over failure like a giant, speaking all the ugly thoughts that shatter and destroy one's self-image. But we are called to hear a different drumbeat. Our failure, given to God, can be raw material for Him to chart another path and open another door. All He needs is our relinquishment of the failure, and our willingness to go forward in obedience to His next chapter for life. Haack reminds us, "The Lord has promised to return soon. Until then, we are to be faithful. That means faithfulness with wealth, fame, power, self-fulfillment and appearance—or without them."[12]

The key phrase expressed here is "or without them." Success is easy to handle. When things are going well, faithfulness seems easy to identify and implement. But failure brings a different environment. Failure brings guilt, self-doubts, and resentment. Failure makes us feel unworthy of God's care and help. What we need to remember is that we are no less the persons in failure than we were in success—unless, of course, sin and disobedience cause the failure.

While we are no less persons, we are fractured beings because of sin. The good steward faces a hard task when failure comes. One must pick up the pieces, give them to God, and see what God's next marching orders are for life. We need to know that failure is not necessarily sinful, nor does it keep us from God's grace and compassion.

Shelley Chapin's life was arrested early by cancer. The dreams and successes faded, and failure seemed the only appropriate word to summarize the journey. But Shelley fought back, using what life had dealt to her for the glory of God. She wrote toward the end of her ordeal:

> I was to learn that all of life depends on grace. Each breath I take, every song I sing, every prayer I offer, and every plan I make—all grow out of grace. . . . Learning to see our lives as a gift, one day at a time, is an important part of living in this world.[13]

One way the steward of God handles failure is to shift the focus from success to service. If what we had offered to God comes to failure, He is Partner with us in the failure. He will not leave us there to drown in self-pity and remorse. He will not abandon us if we are faithful.

This forces a fresh examination of our efforts, our disciplines, and our accountability on these issues. Not all failure is ours; nor is all failure the fault of another. Somewhere there needs to be a place where we process all of it with God and ready ourselves for the journey onward.

Albert Einstein, toward the end of his life, removed portraits of two scientists—Newton and Maxwell—from his wall. He replaced them with portraits of Gandhi and Schweitzer. He explained that it was time to replace the image of success with the image of service.

As Christian stewards, let us keep before us the image of service—service to Christ and His kingdom. Such an image provides a proper view of success. But more important, it gives interpretation and comfort in failure.

Success is not to be measured in material terms nor in popularity and position. Rather, it is best measured in terms of lives touched for good, missions fulfilled for others, and service rendered on behalf of a worthy cause.

Failure is the last word only for the person who is willing to settle for it. For others it is a passage, a moment, an event on the way to a final victory or a success.

Therefore, I urge you, brothers, in view of God's mercy, to offer your bodies as living sacrifices, holy and pleasing to God—this is your spiritual act of worship. Do not conform any longer to the pattern of this world, but be transformed by the renewing of your mind. Then you will be able to test and approve what God's will is—his good, pleasing and perfect will *(Rom. 12:1-2).*

Now it is required that those who have been given a trust must prove faithful *(1 Cor. 4:2).*

9

Stewardship Is Life-size

Stewardship is life-size—it does not end with paying the tithe. As good stewards, no part of our lives can be untouched. Talents, time, attitudes, actions, resources, relationships, mission, suffering, work, leisure—the list goes on and on.

The Stewardship of Relationships

We have seen that because many equate stewardship with the material side of life, other important areas are neglected. Perhaps the biggest gap is in the area of relationships. God brings people into our lives to enrich us, to teach us, and to extend our influence. Relationships are opportunities for stewardship rather than exploitation.

Harvey Potthoff, in his book, *Loneliness*, stated, "Success is not simply a matter of external achievement; it includes the sense of satisfaction in being true to our real self in responsible relationships to others."[1] One of the vital ingredients for healthy Christian living is a caring heart. An ancient Jewish story puts caring in perspective:

> Time before time, when the world was young, two brothers shared a field and a mill, each night dividing evenly the grain they had ground together during the day. One brother lived alone; the other had a wife and a large family. Now the single brother thought to himself one day, "It isn't really fair that we divide the grain evenly. I have only myself to care for, but my brother has children to feed." So each night he secretly took some of his grain to his brother's granary to see that he was never without. But the married

brother said to himself one day, "It isn't really fair that we divide the grain evenly, because I have children to provide for me in my old age, but my brother has no one. What will he do when he is old?" So every night he secretly took some of his grain to his brother's granary. As a result, both of them always found their supply of grain mysteriously replenished each morning.

Then one night they met each other halfway between their two houses, suddenly realized what had been happening, and embraced each other in love.[2]

Stewardship means that one cares about those whom God brings into one's life, by whatever means. How one responds, cares, and reacts to a relationship is a vital part of Christian living. Robert Fulghum, in his book *All I Really Need to Know I Learned in Kindergarten,* writes about a famous French criminologist, Emile Locard, who came up with something he called Locard's Exchange Principle. "It says something to the effect that any person passing through a room will unknowingly deposit something there and take something away." Fulghum's Exchange Principle is extended to read: "Every person passing through this life will unknowingly leave something and take something away."[3]

It is a reminder that no person passes through the world unnoticed. We are contributing something of what God has given to us, and we are receptacles of that which others give. In the repertoire of stewardship our relationships must be given consideration. No person lives in a vacuum. All we have to give—money, talent, ideas, things, love, time, etc.—is given in the context of others.

The gifts of God are best understood in the context of relationship. Money given to the homeless is not only a financial donation, though it is that. In a larger, more meaningful way it is extending the gift of God (money) to one in need. Jesus said, "I tell you the truth, whatever you did for one of the least of these brothers of mine, you did for me" (Matt. 25:40). It is in such giving that God is glorified through His gift.

Such an interpretation is constantly challenged from a world where the secular mind-set has its base. A self-oriented society knows nothing of biblical stewardship. Secular writers and the people of voice and popularity all too often promote a self-first philosophy. In a recent *USA Today,* the summary of a book, *The Dirty Half Dozen: Six Radical Rules to Make Relationships Last,* was given. The rules were:

Don't keep the romance alive. You can't; stop trying.

Don't fight fair. Just don't fight. Give in. Most things in your relationship aren't worth fighting over.

Don't talk about everything. Being totally honest usually makes matters worse.

Don't always tell the truth. That requires total honesty and infinite tact. Both are impossible. Lie some.

Don't let go of the money. Whoever controls it controls the relationship. Split it into two accounts; pay expenses from both equally.

Don't worry about what you think is important. Worry about little things; they're what can do you in.[4]

Such conclusions fly in the face of responsible thinking. Relationship, in such a context, is viewed as selfish endeavor in a "What's in it for me?" attitude. Trust, commitment, care, and all the other ingredients that nurture a relationship are missing. In a world like ours, we must be careful that such an attitude does not erode our outlook. The advice of Vallet is pertinent at this point: "A vital sign of a Christian steward is the willingness to let the ferment of God's actions work freely in your life."[5]

Other Facets of Stewardship

Rebecca Laird has stated, "Good stewardship begins with making wise choices that consider the future usefulness of God's resources rather than just the gratification of our instant desires."[6] Our exercise of these privileges affects others in dramatic ways. Our choices and actions must consider their good as well as ours. Someone observed, "Our behavior . . . influences others for good or ill. We then are stewards of influence and integrity."[7]

There are several areas where our decisions play a vital and lasting part:

—Our ethical stance conveys to others, especially our families, our deep priorities and values. Our ethics and priorities give our children their first training for life. In a subtle but substantial way we are establishing patterns and principles for them, and for others. Such areas call for faithfulness to truth and conviction.

—Our care for the environment and participation in preservation affects those who will come after us. A *USA Today* headline read "Stewardship Embraces Conservation." It quoted a church official as stating, "The whole earth and all its people are threatened with destruction. We confess that this results from human failure to discharge faithfully the responsibility of stewardship."[8] Velva Lorenz reminds us, "Every steward of Christ should feel concern for the land in which we live, remembering with awe and thankfulness, 'The earth is the Lord's, and everything in it' (Ps. 24:1)."[9] The care and preservation of the environment is a part of our responsibility.

—Our stewardship of our bodies affects others. The abuse of the body and mind, through alcohol, drugs, and illicit sex—to name a few—has wide-ranging effect on relationships and families. Some of the deepest heartaches the world knows come from poor use of the body.

A Concluding Word

There is an old maxim that says, "All unhappiness is caused by attachment." In one's quest to be an adequate steward, it is the attachment that creates the biggest struggle. Attachments to things, people, ideas, desires, and self are only a few. The battle one faces is a war between what is right and what one wants. I read these words from Roy L. Smith in a church bulletin: "There is an area of life within which each man is the final authority, and that is in the realm of his own will. For the exercise of that will, each individual is responsible. He is his own steward."[10]

Yes, we are our own stewards before God. Dr. William McCumber reminds us, "We cannot escape stewardship. We do not choose to be stewards; stewardship is structured into our very nature. It comes with the territory of being human. We can only choose to be good or bad stewards, faithful or disloyal stewards."[11]

Stewardship asks us to examine our lives, our values, our priorities, our treasures; indeed, all of life. Stewardship is an initiation to place all things in eternal perspective. Our stewardship needs the kind of reflection of which Henry David Thoreau wrote:

> I went to the woods because I wished to live deliberately, to confront only the essential facts of life, and see if I could not learn what it had to teach, and not, when I came to die, discover that I had not lived . . . I wanted to live deep and suck out all the marrow of life, to live so sturdily and Spartanlike as to put to rout all that was not life, to cut a broad swath and shave close, to drive life into a corner, and reduce it to its lowest terms.[12]

Everyone seeking authentic stewardship needs what Dr. Richard Spindle calls a "breath of fresh air." He writes:

> The breath of God was the first breath to give us life and to create within us that spiritual capacity to recognize and respond to God. There is a human tendency, however, to get busy and grow away from God and get out of breath. More and more we begin to rely on ourselves and our own strength and wisdom. We begin to collect and surround ourselves with toys and stuff. In spite of all our trappings of affluence, we are a culture of self-absorbed, worried, hollow people. Gasping for "a breath of fresh air," we hit bottom before we are forced to look up to the Author of life and breath.[13]

The last word, then, for the steward is that there must be a genuine commitment to God that governs our decisions. We must bring all of life into alignment with His plan and purpose for our lives. William McCumber wrote:

> The acid test of stewardship is the strength of our commitment to the will of God. If we treat our lives and our assets as our own business, to do with as we please, we usurp the right of God.[14]

As we prepare our agenda of stewardship, let us remember that we will give an account, someday, of how we used and invested the gifts of God. Velva Lorenz summed up the concept of stewardship when she wrote:

> The final truth for us is this: As managers, we are entrusted with Spirit-given gifts to be used faithfully and wisely. We receive the grace of God and are rewarded, not by how much or how many gifts are given us, but by our faithfulness and vigilance in using them. As His stewards, we offer our very lives in joy and thanksgiving, gladly caring for all that He has assigned to us.[15]

Ambrose, the bishop of Milan, said, "Gratitude is the interest we pay the Father for the lives He has loaned us."[16] Stewardship is our gratitude expressed through faithfulness.

Stewardship is recognizing that God, who created and endowed life with gifts and abilities, still has a claim on life. The good steward is one who recognizes this and responds with proper accounting of their use and nurture.

That steward who recognizes his indebtedness to the Creator, and his responsibility to others, will orchestrate his abilities and gifts in such a way that both his Creator and his fellowman will be served, and his own soul will be enriched.

Notes

Chapter 1

1. Lou Mobley and Kate McKeown, *Beyond IBM* (New York: McGraw-Hill Publishing Co., 1989), 30.

2. Robert H. Bork, *The Tempting of America: The Political Seduction of the Law* (New York: Free Press, 1990), 10.

3. Ernest Boyer, *The Blackboard Fumble* (Wheaton, Ill.: Victor Books, 1989), 17.

4. Charles Colson, *Against the Night* (Ann Arbor, Mich.: Servant Publisher, 1989), 10-11.

Chapter 2

1. R. T. Williams, *Relationships in Life* (Kansas City: Nazarene Publishing House, n.d.), 35.

2. Latayne C. Scott, *Time, Talents, Things* (Grand Rapids: Zondervan Publishing House, 1987), 17.

3. Rev. Timothy Smith, President's Report, Michigan District NYI Convention, Sat., July 13, 1991.

Chapter 3

1. Samuel Young, "Stewardship," in *Beacon Dictionary of Theology*, ed. Richard S. Taylor (Kansas City: Beacon Hill Press of Kansas City, 1983), 502.

2. T. A. Kantonen, *A Theology for Christian Stewardship* (Philadelphia: Muhlenberg Press, 1956), 1.

3. Samuel Young, *Giving and Living* (Kansas City: Beacon Hill Press of Kansas City, 1974), 16.

4. Thomas C. Rieke, "The End," *Clergy Journal*, November-December 1988, 24.

5. Ronald E. Vallet, *Stepping Stones of the Steward* (Grand Rapids: Wm. B. Eerdmans Publishing Co., 1989), 61.

6. Scott, *Time, Talents, Things*, 11-12.

7. Thomas C. Rieke, "Holy Habits," *Clergy Journal*, February 1989, 16.

8. Vallet, *Stepping Stones*, 4.

9. Eugene H. Peterson, *The Contemplative Pastor* (Carol Stream, Ill.: Christianity Today, 1989), 12.

10. J. Kerby Anderson, ed., *Living Ethically in the 90's* (Wheaton, Ill.: Victor Books, 1990), 44.

Chapter 4

1. Myron Rush, *Lord of the Marketplace* (Wheaton, Ill.: Victor Books, 1986), 11.

2. Steven Harper, *Embrace the Spirit* (Wheaton, Ill.: Victor Books, 1987), 57.

3. William Arthur Ward, *Thoughts of a Christian Optimist* (Anderson, S.C.: Droxe House Publisher, 1968), 79.

4. J. Grant Howard, *Balancing Life's Demands* (Portland, Oreg.: Multnomah Press, 1983), 19.

5. Thomas C. Rieke, "High Time," *Clergy Journal*, April 1988, 36.

6. Scott, *Time, Talents, Things*, 39.

7. Ibid., 43.

Chapter 5

1. Williams, *Relationships in Life*, 38.

2. Richard Lee Spindle, *A Breath of Fresh Air* (Kansas City: Beacon Hill Press of Kansas City, 1989), 101.

3. John Bartlett, *Familiar Quotations*, 13th ed. (Boston: Little, Brown, and Co., 1955), 861.

4. Spindle, *Breath of Fresh Air*, 49.

5. Richard Austin Thompson, "Stewardship," *Clergy Journal*, July 1991, 37.

6. Scott, *Time, Talents, Things*, 11.

7. Donald B. Krabill, *The Upside-Down Kingdom* (Scottdale, Pa.: Herald Press, 1978), 147.

8. Bob Benson and Michael W. Benson, *Disciplines for the Inner Life* (Waco, Tex.: Word Books, 1986), 59.

9. William Wells, *The Agony of Affluence* (Grand Rapids: Zondervan Publishing House, 1989), 17.

Chapter 6

1. George Barna, *The Frog in the Kettle* (Ventura, Calif.: Regal Books, 1990), 23.

2. Bill Hull, *The Disciple-Making Pastor* (Old Tappan, N.J.: Fleming H. Revell, 1988), 42.

3. Ibid.

4. Ibid.

5. Ibid., 43.

6. Stephen D. Eyre, "The Dragon of Materialism," in *Clean Living in a Dirty World,* ed., Stephen M. Miller (Kansas City: Beacon Hill Press of Kansas City, 1991), 65.

7. Bob Shank, *Total Life Management* (Portland, Oreg.: Multnomah Press, 1990), 97.

8. Vallet, *Stepping Stones*, 51.

9. Spindle, *Breath of Fresh Air*, 101.

10. C. Peter Wagner, *Your Spiritual Gifts Can Help Your Church Grow* (Ventura, Calif.: Regal Books, 1979), 52.

11. Allan Cox, *Straight Talk for Monday Morning* (New York: Jolin Wiltey and Sons, 1990), 84.

12. Ibid.

13. Ibid.

Chapter 7

1. Denis Haack, *The Rest of Success* (Downers Grove, Ill.: InterVarsity Press, 1989), 113.

2. Ibid., 117.

3. Ibid., 126.

4. Ibid., 127.

5. Leland Ryken, *Worldly Saints: The Puritans as They Really Were* (Grand Rapids: Zondervan Publishing House, 1986), 37.

6. Darius Salter, "Our Vocation: Ministry," *Sounding Board* (Summer 1986): 2.

7. Haack, *The Rest of Success*, 127.

8. Harper, *Embrace the Spirit*, 49.

9. Ibid., 63.

10. Peterson, *The Contemplative Pastor*, 21.

11. Richard I. Winwood, *Excellence Through Time Management* (Salt Lake City: Franklin Institute, 1985), 10.

12. Earl Palmer, *Signposts* (Dallas: Word Books, 1990), 72-73.

Chapter 8

1. Williams, *Relationships in Life*, 6.

2. Palmer, *Signposts*, 161.

3. Thomas C. Rieke, "Youth Are Stewards," *Clergy Journal*, April 1989, 17.

4. Linda Eyre and Richard Eyre, *Life Balance* (New York: Ballantine Books, 1987), 33.

5. Haack, *Rest of Success*, 67.

6. Ibid., 103.

7. Ibid., 105.

8. Henri J. M. Nouwen, *In the Name of Jesus* (New York: Crossroad, 1989), 3-4.

9. Ibid., 10.

10. Haack, *Rest of Success*, 140.

11. Alex MacKenzie, *Time for Success* (New York: McGraw-Hill Publishing Co., 1989), 8.

12. Haack, *Rest of Success*, 102-3.

13. Shelley Chapin, *Within the Shadow* (Wheaton, Ill.: Victor Books, 1991), 16.

Chapter 9

1. Harvey H. Potthoff, *Loneliness* (Nashville: Abingdon Press, 1976), 58.

2. Vallet, *Stepping Stones*, 20.

3. Robert Fulghum, *All I Really Need to Know I Learned in Kindergarten* (New York: Ivy Books, 1986), 117.

4. Anita Manning, "Keeping Sparks Alive Can Burn Out a Marriage," *USA Today*, Aug. 27, 1991, D-1.

5. Vallet, *Stepping Stones*, 154.

6. Rebecca Laird, "The Simple Life in a Complex World," in *Clean Living in a Dirty World*, ed. Stephen M. Miller (Kansas City: Beacon Hill Press of Kansas City, 1991), 53.

7. Boyer, *Blackboard Fumble*, 32.

8. "Stewardship Embraces Conservation," *USA Today*, Feb. 28, 1990, 60.

9. Velva Lorenz, "Stewardship: What Is It?" *Preacher's Magazine*, September/October/November 1991, 34.

10. Bulletin, Grand Ledge, Mich., Church of the Nazarene, Jan. 27, 1991.

11. W. E. McCumber, "Inescapable," *Herald of Holiness*, January 1991, 31.

12. Spindle, *Breath of Fresh Air*, 36.

13. Ibid., 90-91.

14. McCumber, "Inescapable," 31.

15. Lorenz, "Stewardship," 36.

16. Quoted in *Illustration Digest*, November-December 1989, 2.

Bibliography
Recommended for Further Reading

Fisher, Wallace. *A New Climate for Stewardship*. Nashville: Abingdon Press, 1976.

Foster, Richard J. *Freedom of Simplicity*. San Francisco: Harper and Row, 1981.

———. *Money, Sex, and Power*. San Francisco: Harper and Row, 1985.

Goodwin, J. W. *Tithing: The Touchstone of Stewardship*. Kansas City: Nazarene Publishing House, n.d.

Hall, Douglas John. *The Steward: A Biblical Symbol Come of Age*. New York: Friendship Press, 1982.

———. *The Stewardship of Life in the Kingdom of Death*. Grand Rapids: Wm. B. Eerdmans Publishing Co., 1985.

Perkins, Phyllis H. *The Bible Speaks to Me About My Service and Mission*. Kansas City: Beacon Hill Press of Kansas City, 1990.

Smith, Harold Ivan. *The Jabez Principle: A Christian Perspective of Work and Lifestyle*. Kansas City: Beacon Hill Press of Kansas City, 1987.

Spruce, Fletcher C., and James R. Spruce. *You Can Be a Joyful Tither*. Kansas City: Beacon Hill Press of Kansas City, 1985.

Stockton, John. *Investments Here and Hereafter*. Kansas City: Nazarene Publishing House, 1964.

Wolf, Earl C. *Tithing Is for Today*. Kansas City: Beacon Hill Press of Kansas City, 1981.